"I can't imagine anything worse"

A salute to Prince Philip
(in his own words)

Published by OH!
20 Mortimer Street
London W1T 3JW

Disclaimer:

ISBN 978-1-80069-071-4

Compiled by: Malcolm Croft
Editorial: Lisa Dyer, Stella Caldwell
Project manager: Russell Porter
Design: Tony Seddon
Production: Freencky Portas

A CIP catalogue record for this book is available from the British Library

Printed in Dubai

10 9 8 7 6 5 4 3 2 1

Cover photograph: Samir Hussein/WireImage/Getty Images

"I can't imagine anything worse"

A salute to Prince Philip
(in his own words)

OH!

Contents

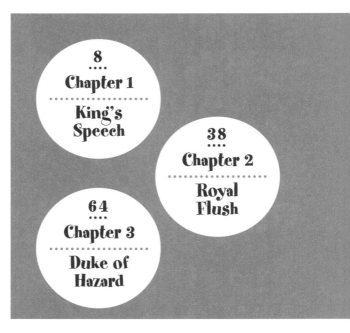

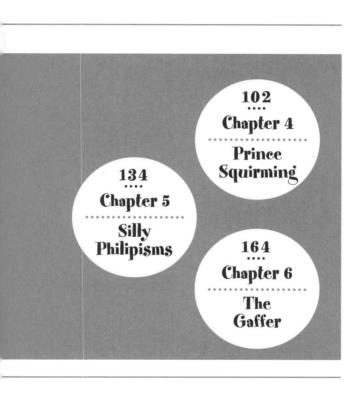

Introduction

If it seems like Prince Philip has been around forever, then his age certainly proves it. No matter what people may think of him – or more importantly the words that have slipped out of his mouth – one thing is clear: the Duke is an icon of the royal family and a reminder of a time when the world was a different place.

For all of Philip's "gaffes", "blunders", "off-the-cuff remarks" – or any other euphemism you care to think of – he has done his best, in all his long years of royal service, to keep the monarchy memorable, relevant, human even. To his family, he may have been an occasional thorn in the side, but to the public he has been the thorn that has pricked and tickled their attention every time they started to forget the monarchy was still even there.

For as rude, senseless or derogatory as many of Philip's wisecracks and quips have appeared – as you'll see inside these pages – at the root of this royal is a very funny man who, seemingly, never took life too seriously. And for that, the British public have come to embrace him as that embarrassing/harmless/charming uncle type at weddings who can get a bit lairy and out of control. Of course, it's those people that make you remember the moment – and you really do miss them when they're no longer there...

So that is precisely why this salute to Prince Philip is here: the perfect pocket-sized companion – call it a souvenir – of perhaps the only member of the royal family who has ever seemed real (and who perhaps could have been a stand-up comedian in another life). This tiny tome is a celebration of his extraordinary life in the service of his subjects, as well a compilation of his best (and worst) one-liners, in his own imitable style.

Enjoy…!

"I can't imagine **anything** worse"

· · · · · · · · · · · ·

Chapter 1

King's Speech

Philip, prince, earl, duke, baron, king – no matter what you call him, one thing is clear: he loves to playfully engage with his subjects. Even if it doesn't always go according to royal etiquette...

King's Speech

66

Dentopedalogy is the science of opening your mouth and putting your foot in it. I have been practising it for years.

99

Philip, in an address to
the Dental Council Meeting, 1960.

66

I know I am rude.
But it's fun.

99

Philip, 1942 (at the age of 21).

King's Speech

66

I rather doubt whether anyone
has ever been genuinely shocked
by anything I have said.

99

Philip, in an interview, 1999.

66

We live in what virtually amounts
to a museum – which does not
happen to a lot of people.

99

Philip, about Buckingham Palace, 1964.

King's Speech

> **❝**
>
> Well, that's more than
> you know about anything
> else then.
>
> **❞**

Philip, speaking to the beloved BBC newsreader,
Michael Buerk, after being told by him that he know nothing
about the Duke of Edinburgh's Gold Awards, 2004.

"

My son owns them.

"

Philip, having been asked during a Canadian tour whether he "knew of the Scilly Isles", 2010.

King's Speech

“

What the hell are they playing at?

”

Philip, after hearing of Prince Harry and Meghan Markle's plans to cease all royal duties, 2020.

Smashing Fact No.1

Philip was 13 years old when he met his future wife, Elizabeth. They were both attending the wedding of Princess Marina of Greece and the Duke of Kent in 1934. Elizabeth was eight at the time. The pair met again five years later.

King's Speech

66

Every time I talk to a woman they say I've been to bed with her. Well, I'm bloody flattered at my age to think some girl is interested in me. It's absolutely cuckoo.

99

Philip, discussing his "womanizing" claims, to BBC interviewer Jeremy Paxman, 2006.

"

I reckon I have done something right if I don't appear in the media. So I've retreated – quite consciously – so as not to be an embarrassment.

"

Philip, discussing his reduced royal visibility, to BBC interviewer Jeremy Paxman, 2006.

King's Speech

66

I would be arrested if I unzipped that dress.

99

Philip, to a well-wisher in Bromley (who was wearing a dress with a vertical zip on the front), during a Diamond Jubilee visit with the Queen, 2012.

66

Who do you sponge off?

99

*Philip, speaking with a group of women at a Chadwell Heath
Community Centre in Barking and Dagenham, 2015.*

King's Speech

> **"**
>
> I hear you're an actor? Well,
> I was given a DVD player for
> Christmas and I can't work out
> whether I put the green cord
> in or the red cord.
>
> **"**

*Philip, to Academy Award-winning actor Cate Blanchett
when she told him she worked "in the film industry", 2008.*

"
Yak, yak, yak.
Come on... get a move on.
"

Philip, to the Queen, from the deck of HMY Britannia in Belize, 1994. (Elizabeth was on the dock talking to her hosts.)

King's Speech

66

Is that a terrorist?

99

Philip, pointing towards a tall man with a bushy ginger beard while walking to Sandringham's St Mary Magdalene Church, 2017.

"

Wind farms are absolutely useless and an absolute disgrace.

"

Philip, speaking to Esbjorn Wilmar,
a managing director of a wind farm*, 2011.

*Mr Wilmar suggested that the Duke put wind turbines on his estate. Philip
replied: "You stay away from my estate, young man!"

King's Speech

"

If the man had succeeded in abducting Anne, she would have given him a hell of a time while in captivity.

"

Philip, after a gunman was foiled trying to kidnap his daughter, the Princess Royal, 1974.

66

I declare this thing open,
whatever it is.

99

Philip, during a state visit to Canada, 1969.

King's Speech

"

Are you asking me if the Queen is going to die?

"

Philip, being asked when the Prince of Wales would succeed to the throne, 2017.

66

God, I don't want to live to
be a hundred, I can't imagine
anything worse.

99

Philip, on his centenary, to biographer Gyles Brandreth, 2004.

King's Speech

66

I'm not going to be drawn into speculating on that. All I'll say is that I've tried to help keep it going while I've been here.

99

Philip, on the future of the monarchy, and whether Charles will become king, to biographer Gyles Brandreth, 2004.

"

Where was home? Wherever I happened to be. It was no great deal. I just lived my life.

"

Philip, on the subject of his dysfunctional childhood, for a BBC documentary, 2011.

King's Speech

> **"**
>
> I was not the least aware I was any different from any of the other [schoolchildren]. It's true I had this title of Prince, but it's surprising how you can live it down.
>
> **"**

Philip, reflecting on his schooldays, 2011.

66

Still downtrodden, then?

99

Philip, at a women's centre in Hull, 2009.

King's Speech

66

You can't have been here
that long – you haven't got
a pot belly.

99

Philip, to a British tourist during a tour of Budapest, 1993.

Keep your heads above water.

Philip, to Hull City council leader, following a day meeting victims of flooding that decimated large parts of the city, 2009.

King's Speech

66

How do you keep the natives
off the booze long enough to
pass the test?

99

Philip, to a Scottish driving instructor, 1995.

66

Ah! You're the one who
wrote the letter. So you can
write then?
Ha, ha! Well done.

99

*Philip, during a meeting with a teenager who had invited the
Queen to visit Essex, 2003.*

"I can't imagine **anything** worse"

. . . .

Chapter 2

Royal Flush

According to those who know the prince, they consider him a quick wit and as sharp as a pin, even if sometimes his intellect got the better of him.
You have been warned!

Royal Flush

"

In the first years of the Queen's reign, the level of adulation – you wouldn't believe it, you really wouldn't. It could have been corroding. It would have been very easy to play to the gallery, but I took a conscious decision not to do that.
Safer not to be too popular.
You can't fall too far.

"

Philip, in an interview for his ninetieth birthday, 2011.

66

It looks as though it was put in by an Indian*.

99

Philip offers his opinion of a fuse box during a tour of a Scottish factory, 1999.

*"I meant to say cowboys. I just got my cowboys and Indians mixed up," he later clarified.

Royal Flush

66

Ghastly.

99

Philip's opinion of Beijing, during a 1986 tour of China.

"

It's a vast waste of space.

"

Philip, speaking to 2,000 guests at the reception of a new £18m British Embassy in Berlin, which the Queen had just opened.

Royal Flush

"

If it has four legs and it is
not a chair, if it has got two
wings and it flies but is not
an aeroplane and if it swims
and it is not a submarine, the
Cantonese will eat it.

"

Philip, chairing a World Wildlife Fund meeting, 1986.

❝

There's a lot of your family in tonight.

❞

Philip, to business chief Atul Patel's name badge during a 2009 Buckingham Palace reception for 400 influential British Indians.

Royal Flush

66

You are a woman, aren't you?

99

Philip, to a Kenyan women, after accepting a gift, 1984.

66

You must be
out of your minds.

99

*Philip, to native residents of the Solomon Islands,
after being told that their population growth was five per
cent a year*, 1982.*

*Global averages are one per cent.

Royal Flush

66

Young people are the same
as they always were. They are
just as ignorant.

99

*Philip, during a ceremony for the 50th anniversary of the
Duke of Edinburgh's Awards scheme he founded.*

“

Your country is one of the most notorious centres of trading in endangered species.

”

Philip, after accepting a conservation award in Thailand, 1991.

Royal Flush

66

Aren't most of you descended
from pirates?

99

*Philip, to one of the wealthiest native Caymanians on the
Cayman Islands, 1994.*

So who's on drugs here?...
He **looks as if he's on drugs.**

Philip, to a teenage member of a Bangladeshi youth club, 2002.

Royal Flush

66

I can only repeat what I have said before. If invited, I will always do my utmost to help you and Charles to the best of my ability. But I am quite ready to concede that I have no talent as a marriage counsellor!!!

99

Philip, in a letter to Princess Diana*, following the news of Prince Charles' affair, 1992.

*Diana referred to Philip as "Pa".

Smashing Fact No.2

"He looks like a plum pudding!"

The words uttered by Philip upon the birth of his eldest son, Charles.

Royal Flush

"

During the Blitz a lot
of shops had their windows
blown in and sometimes
they put up notices saying,
'More open than usual.'
I now declare this place more
open than usual.

"

*Philip, while unveiling a plaque at the University of
Hertfordshire's new campus, 2003.*

<blockquote>
"

You have mosquitoes. I have the Press.

"
</blockquote>

Philip, to the matron of a Caribbean hospital, 1966.

Royal Flush

66

Well, you didn't have to come!

99

*Philip, to the then editor-in-chief of the Independent
newspaper, after he had told the Duke he had been invited
to the press reception to mark the Golden Jubilee, 2002.*

66

Ah good, there's so many over there you feel they breed them just to put in orphanages.

99

Philip, to a Duke of Edinburgh's Award recipient when he told the Duke that he was not going to travel to Romania for six months to assist with the Romanian orphan crisis, 2006.

Royal Flush

"

Children go to school because
their parents don't want them
in the house.

"

*Philip, to Malala Yousafzai, the survivor of an assassination
attempt by the Taliban and who now campaigns for the right
of girls to go to school without fear, 2013.*

66

You look like a suicide bomber.

99

Philip, to a young policewoman wearing a bullet-proof vest in Stornoway, 2002.

Royal Flush

66

You look starved.

99

Philip, addressing a pensioner during a visit to the
Charterhouse almshouse for elderly men, 2017.

"

Are you running away from something?

"

Philip, speaking with British expats in Abu Dhabi, 2011.

Royal Flush

66

I'm just a bloody amoeba.
I'm the only man in the country
not to have given his children
his name.

99

*Philip, when the Queen declared the Royal Family's chosen
surname would be Windsor and not Mountbatten, 1952.*

❝
He needs to knuckle down
and not wimp out.
❞

*Philip, on Prince William's unhappiness studying during
university, 2003.*

"I can't imagine anything worse"

Chapter 3

Duke of Hazard

For more than 75 years, the Duke has been entertaining the eyes and ears of England. We will miss him when he's gone... but he won't be forgotten. Largely thanks to these memorable remarks.

Duke of Hazard

66

If people feel it has no further part to play, then for goodness sake, let's end the thing on amicable terms without having a row about it.

99

Philip, discussing the future of the monarchy and the Commonwealth to a Canadian official, 1976.

I have had two books of speeches published, and one on birds. Needless to say, the one on birds was more successful.

Philip, discussing his success in print, 1970.

Duke of Hazard

"

Which are the Press and which are the apes?

"

Philip, at the rock of Gibraltar with the Queen, could not discern between the congregating press corp and the destination's other famous residents, 1954.

66

I hope you are not
going to blow us up with your
concealed bombs.

99

*Philip, to two Irish nuns, who turned up to Buckingham
Palace for a special school outing party for
schoolchildren, 1974.*

Duke of Hazard

"

I am not really a talented
spectator, frankly. Yes, it's
quite fun to watch but it's not
the be-all and end-all. I did
something like five Olympic
Games, as president of the
FEI, when I was just standing
around watching these things.
I'd rather do something.

"

*Philip, in an interview with the Telegraph, on the subject of
the London 2012 Olympics, 2006.*

66

How on earth do you get that under your helmet?

99

Philip, pointing to the turban of a Sikh policeman, at a Christmas party for royal staff at Buckingham Palace, 2003.

Duke of Hazard

"

Lose the feet and get some wheels.

"

Philip jokes with a double amputee, a UK soldier who lost both legs in a bomb blast in Afghanistan, that he should put wheels on his prosthetic limbs, 2016.

"

Just take the fucking picture!

"

*Philip, to an RAF photographer during an official photo
shoot commemorating the 75th anniversary of
the Battle of Britain, 2015.*

Duke of Hazard

66
Are you all one family?
99

Philip meets the multi-ethnic dance troupe Diversity following their routine at the Royal Variety Performance, 2009.

"

Oh, what, a strip club?

"

Philip, to a young Barnstaple female Sea Cadet, who told him she worked as a barmaid in a nightclub, 2010.*

*He then added: "Probably too cold for that anyway."

Duke of Hazard

66

The Philippines must be
half empty, you're all here
running the NHS.

99

*Philip, speaking with a Filipino nurse at Luton and Dunstable
University Hospital, 2016.*

66
You managed not to get
eaten then?
99

*Philip, to a British student who had trekked Papua New
Guinea, during an official visit in 1998.*

Smashing Fact No.3

Philip's bank account had 12 pence in it before he married his wife, Elizabeth, the richest women in England.

"

We don't come here for our health. We can think of other ways of enjoying ourselves.

"

Philip, during a royal state visit to Canada, 1976.

Duke of Hazard

"

A few years ago, everybody was saying we must have more leisure, everyone's working too much. Now that everybody's got more leisure time they are complaining they are unemployed. People don't seem to make up their minds what they want.

"

Philip, discussing Britain's recession, 1981.

66

British women can't cook. They are very good at decorating food and making it attractive. But they have an inability to cook.

99

Philip, addressing a mainly female audience at the Scottish Rural Women's Institute, 1966.

Duke of Hazard

66

It was part of the fortunes of war. We didn't have counsellors rushing around every time somebody let off a gun, asking 'Are you all right – are you sure you don't have a ghastly problem?' You just got on with it!

99

Philip, discussing the subject of counselling for Second World War veterans, 1995.

66

Were you here in the bad old days?... That's why you can't read and write then!

99

Philip, to parents during a visit to a Sheffield comprehensive school with a poor academic reputation.

Duke of Hazard

66

No, I would probably
end up spitting it out over
everybody.

99

*Philip declines the offer of a fish supper from seafood chef
Rick Stein's upmarket deli, 2000.*

66

Any bloody fool
can lay a wreath at the
thingamy.

99

*Philip, discussing his royal role during an interview with
BBC presenter Jeremy Paxman, 2006.*

Duke of Hazard

66

Holidays are curious things, aren't they? You send children to school to get them out of your hair. Then they come back and make life difficult for parents. That is why holidays are set so they are just about the limit of your endurance.

99

Philip, at the opening of a school in 2000.

"

People think there's a rigid class system in England, but dukes have even been known to marry chorus girls. Some have even married Americans.

"

Philip, responding to a journalist's question about marriage, 1997.

Duke of Hazard

66

Can you tell the difference between them?

99

Philip, about David Cameron, Gordon Brown and Dmitry Medvedev, the Russian president, to then-US President Barack Obama at a function ahead of the G20 Summit, 2009.

66

I don't know how they are
going to integrate in places
like Glasgow and Sheffield.

99

Philip, to students from Brunei, shortly after
they arrived in Britain to study, 1998.

Duke of Hazard

"

Do people trip over you?

"

Philip, meeting a wheelchair-bound nursing-home resident, 2002.

66

It looks like a tart's bedroom.

99

*Philip, after having seen the extravagant architectural
plans for the Duke and Duchess of York's house
at Sunninghill Park, 1988.*

Duke of Hazard

66

We go into the red next year...
I shall probably have to give
up polo.

99

*Philip, discussing the Royal Family's finances in an interview
on US television, 1969.*

66

Bugger the table plan, give me
my dinner!

99

Philip, at a dinner party at Buckingham Palace, 2004.

Duke of Hazard

66

I thought it was against the
law these days for a woman
to solicit.

99

Philip, speaking to a female solicitor, 1987.

66

You're just a silly little
Whitehall twit: you don't trust
me and I don't trust you.

99

Philip, to Sir Rennie Maudslay, the Queen's treasurer, 1970.

Duke of Hazard

❝

What about Tom Jones?
He's made a million and he's a
bloody awful singer.

❞

Philip, during a speech at a luncheon focused on the
challenges of becoming wealthy in Britain, 1969.

66

I'd much rather have
stayed in the Navy, frankly.

99

*Philip, discussing his role as a member of the
Royal Family, 1992.*

Duke of Hazard

"

I am rude and unmannerly and I say many things out of turn which I realize afterwards must have hurt someone. Then I am filled with remorse and I try to put matters right.

"

Philip, aged 21, in a letter to the mother whose son, Alex Wernher, had been killed in the Second World War, 1942.

"

I'm not very good at man-
made fibres myself.

"

*Philip, while opening the Man-made Fibres Building
Exhibition in Leeds, commenting on his thinning locks, 1956.*

Duke of Hazard

❝

I don't know. A refugee
husband, I suppose.

❞

*Philip, to his biographer Gyles Brandreth, about how the
Duke is perceived publicly, 2006.*

66

Who cares what I think about it?

99

*Philip, when was asked about his successes, in a
BBC interview to celebrate his ninetieth birthday, 2011.*

"I can't imagine **anything** worse"

. . . .

Chapter 4

Prince Squirming

As it has been said, Prince Philip is the only man on earth to treat the Queen of England as an ordinary person, and has been by her side for more than 70 years. If she can put up with him, so can we…

Prince Squirming

"

And balls to you, sir.

"

Philip's reply to the then-president of the National Bowling Club after a short speech at a banquet. Upon realizing that Prince Philip did not understand the speech, he made an effort to summon up his entire English vocabulary when presenting the emblem of the club to the prince and said: "Balls, you know".

66

I wish he'd turn the
microphone off!

99

*Philip, during Elton John's performance at the 73rd
Royal Variety Show, 2001.*

Prince Squirming

"

Do you still throw spears
at each other?

"

*Philip, speaking to an Aboriginal leader at the Aboriginal
Cultural Park in Queensland, 2002.*

66

Where's the Southern Comfort?

99

Philip, having been presented with a hamper of southern delicacies by the US ambassador in London, 1999.

Prince Squirming

66

That's a nice tie...
Do you have any knickers in
that material?

99

*Philip, to then-Scottish Conservative leader, Annabel Goldie,
discussing the tartan to be used for the Pope's forthcoming
state visit, 2010.*

❝

Get me a beer.
I don't care what kind it is, just
get me a beer!

❞

*Philip, after being offered a fine Italian wine by Prime Minister
Giuliano Amato at a state dinner, 2000.*

Prince Squirming

"

If a cricketer, for instance, suddenly decided to go into a school and batter a lot of people to death with a cricket bat, which he could do very easily, I mean, are you going to ban cricket bats?

"

Philip, during a radio interview, shortly after the Dunblane shootings, 1996.*

*Off-air after the interview, Philip told the interviewer, "That will really set the cat among the pigeons, won't it?"

66

I would like to go to Russia very much – although the bastards murdered half my family.

99

Philip, after being asked by a journalist if he would like to visit the Soviet Union, 1967.

Prince Squirming

"

I don't think a prostitute is
more moral than a wife, but
they are doing the same thing.

"

*Philip, using an analogy to discuss meat slaughter
and blood sports, 1988.*

"

Ah, so this is feminist
corner then.

"

*Philip, walking towards a group of female Labour MPs (all
of whom were wearing name badges reading "Ms") at a
Buckingham Palace drinks reception, 2000.*

Prince Squirming

> 66
>
> Cats kill far more birds than men.
> Why don't you have a slogan:
> 'Kill a cat and save a bird'?
>
> 99

Philip, discussing the Turtle Doves Protection Project in Anguilla, 1965.

66

All money nowadays seems
to be produced with a natural
homing instinct for the Treasury.

99

Philip, highlighting the increasing rate of British tax, 1963.

Prince Squirming

66

It is my invariable custom to say something flattering to begin with so that I shall be excused if by any chance I put my foot in it later on.

99

Philip, delivering a speech, 1956.

66

Why don't you go and live in a
hostel to save cash?

99

Philip, speaking to a less-than-affluent student, 1998.

Smashing Fact No.4

When first introduced to King George, Elizabeth's father, at Balmoral, Philip was forced to wear a kilt. As a joke, Philip curtsied, instead of bowing. The King did not find it funny.

"
Ghastly place, isn't it?
"

Philip's opinion of Stoke-on-Trent to the city's Labour then-MP Joan Walley, 1997.

Prince Squirming

"

Deaf? If you're near there, no
wonder you are deaf.

"

*Philip to a group of deaf children standing near a Caribbean
steel drum band, 2000.*

"

If you stay here much longer, you will go home with slitty eyes.

"

Philip, to a 21-year-old British student during a visit to China, 1986.

Prince Squirming

66

Oh, it's you that owns that ghastly car, is it? We often see it when driving to Windsor Castle.

99

Philip, to neighbour Elton John, after hearing John had sold his Watford FC-themed (yellow, with a red and black stripe in the middle) Aston Martin, 2001.

66

Do you know they have eating
dogs for the anorexic now?

99

*Philip, to a blind, wheelchair-bound person, and
their guide dog, 2002.*

Prince Squirming

"

The problem with London is the tourists. They cause the congestion. If we could just stop the tourism, we could stop the congestion.

"

Philip, at the opening of London's new City Hall building, 2002.

❝

A pissometer?

❞

Philip renamed the piezometer water gauge, following a demonstration by an Australian farmer, 2000.

Prince Squirming

"

I have never been noticeably reticent about talking on subjects about which I know nothing.

"

Philip, while addressing a group of industrialists, 1961.

66

It's not a very big one, but
at least it's dead and it took an
awful lot of killing!

99

Philip, discussing the crocodile he had shot while in
Gambia, 1957.

Prince Squirming

66

Well, you didn't design your beard too well, did you? If you are going to grow a beard, grow a beard. You really must try harder.

99

Philip, to a young fashion designer at a Buckingham Palace reception, 2009.

Smashing Fact No.5

At breakfast on the morning of his wedding to Queen Elizabeth, Prince Philip and his best man David Milford Haven drank gin and tonics.

Prince Squirming

> **"**
> In the event that I am
> reincarnated, I would like
> to return as a deadly virus,
> to contribute something to
> solving overpopulation.
> **"**

Philip, in the foreword to the book If I Were an Animal, *1987.*

66

Have you run over anybody?

99

Philip, to the Mayor of Waltham Forest, Geoff Walker, who uses a mobility scooter, 2012.

Prince Squirming

"

I can only assume it is largely
due to the accumulation of
toasts to my health over the
years that I am still enjoying
a fairly satisfactory state of
health and have reached such
an unexpectedly great age.

"

*Philip, in a speech to the Corporation of the City of London,
to celebrate his 80th birthday, 2001.*

66

You must have really good
brains to speak Welsh.

99

Philip, to school children in Cardiff, 2012.

"I can't imagine anything worse"

Chapter 5

Silly Philipisms

You know you've become famous for your words when you get an "-ism" after your name. Indeed, the phenomenon of "Philipisms" is alive and well and will be long remembered after the Duke sadly shuffles off his mortal coil. These are some of his best…

Silly Philipisms

❝

The EU is all balls.

❞

Philip to a Labour Euro MP, 2004.

66

You're about to see
the world's most experienced
plaque-unveiler.

99

*Philip, unveiling the new £25m Warner Stand at
Lord's Cricket Ground, 2017.*

Silly Philipisms

“

He's younger than I am, funnily enough. He may not look it.

”

Philip, about Prince Charles, to Terry Wogan, 1991.

Smashing Fact No.6

When the time comes, Philip will have a private military-style commemoration in St George's Chapel at Windsor Castle, and not a state funeral, as he is entitled. "I don't want all the fuss," he said. He will buried in Frogmore Gardens, along with several other Mountbattens.

Silly Philipisms

66

I am interested in leisure the
same way as a poor man is
interested in money – I can't
get enough of it.

99

Philip, on the subject of his royal role, 1984.

“

I don't see her because I don't see much point.

”

Philip, about Sarah Ferguson, 1999.

Silly Philipisms

> **66**
>
> For the past forty years I have never moved anywhere without a policeman accompanying me. So how the hell could I get away with anything like that?
>
> **99**

Philip, to a journalist, on the subject of his alleged infidelity, 1992.

> **"**
> They're a damn nuisance!
> I've got one in my bathroom
> and every time I run my bath
> the steam sets it off.
> **"**

Philip, discussing smoke alarms to a woman who lost two sons in a fire, 1998.

Silly Philipisms

"

Where did you get that hat?

"

*Philip, reunited with the Queen at the door of
Westminster Abbey at the end of the coronation,
referring to her crown, 1953.*

66

You look like you're ready
for bed!

99

*Philip, to the President of Nigeria, Olusegun Obasanjo, who
was dressed in traditional robes, 2003.*

Silly Philipisms

> **"**
> When a man opens a car door
> for his wife, it's either a new car
> or a new wife.
> **"**

Philip, discussing marriage, 1988.

66

Are we going to need
ear plugs?

99

Philip, after hearing that Madonna sang the film's
theme song at the Royal World Premiere of the Bond movie,
Die Another Day, 2002.

Smashing Fact No.7

In 1972, Philip requested that the design of the new 50p coin be altered so that it read "pence" in full. "I don't like that little 'p'," he said.

66

Have you ever flown in a plane?
Well, it was just like that.

99

Philip, when asked "What was your flight like, your Royal Highness?" by an official greeting him at a Canadian airport, 2000.

Silly Philipisms

"

Bring back Mrs T, that's
what I say. There's no one quite
like Mrs T.

"

Philip, during the Blair Labour years, circa 2005.

66

If you don't walk, I think you'll regret it later.

99

Philip, to teenage Prince William, on whether to walk behind Princess Diana's coffin during the funeral procession.

*William did; and the image is now iconic.

Silly Philipisms

66

My favourite subject at school was avoiding unnecessary work.

99

Philip quipped while playing bicycle polo on Smiths Lawn in Windsor Park, 1967.

66

Oh! You are the people ruining
the rivers and the environment.

99

*Philip addressing three employees of a Holyrood
fish farm, 1999.*

Silly Philipisms

"

If you travel as much as
we do, you appreciate the
improvements in aircraft design
of less noise and more comfort
– provided you don't travel
in something called economy
class, which sounds ghastly.

"

Philip, speaking to the Aircraft Research Association, 2002.

66

French cooking's all very well,
but they can't do a decent
English breakfast.

99

*Philip, after eating a breakfast of bacon, eggs, smoked
salmon, kedgeree, croissants and pain au chocolat, made by
French top chef Régis Crépy, 2002.*

Silly Philipisms

66

You're not wearing mink
knickers, are you?

99

*Philip, speaking to a fashion editor at a World Wildlife Fund
gathering, 1993.*

66

You were playing your
instruments? Or do you have
tape recorders under
your seats?

99

Philip, to musicians in an Australian school orchestra, 2002.

Silly Philipisms

66

It's a pleasure to be in a country that isn't ruled by its people.

99

Philip, to then-Paraguay dictator General Stroessner, 1963.

Smashing Fact No.8

It was only when Philip enquired why royal staff left a bottle of Scotch in Queen Elizabeth's bedroom every night, that its purpose was revealed. Queen Victoria had once asked for a bottle of Scotch to be left in her room to combat a cold. The order was simply never rescinded.

Silly Philipisms

66

I'm sorry officer, but I've got
an appointment with the
Archbishop of Canterbury.

99

*Philip, when stopped by a police officer for speeding through
central London on 19 November 1947, on route to a final
rehearsal of the royal wedding. He married Princess Elizabeth
the next day.*

66

We shall all be old one
day – provided, of course, we
can avoid being slaughtered
on the roads or beaten up
by some hooligan in a peace
demonstration.

99

Philip, reflecting on old age, 1970.

Silly Philipisms

66

I'm not sure I recommend it. It's not so much the age, but trying to survive the celebrations.

99

Philip, on turning 80, 2001.

"

Well I can't stand up much longer.

"

Philip, to Sir Michael Atiyah, during at a reception for members of the Order of Merit at St James's Palace, 2017, regarding the Duke's royal retirement. Atiyah had said, "I'm sorry to hear you're standing down."

"I can't imagine anything worse"

Chapter 6

The Gaffer

For years, Philip's love of putting a cat among the pigeons was largely regarded as the Duke himself making "blunders". But the truth is much more innocent. He just wanted to put his subjects at ease when they met his looming presence, and a joke fit the bill, even if it would sometimes flop. Or cause an international diplomatic controversy.

The Gaffer

66

And what exotic part of the
world do you come from?

99

*Philip, addressing Conservative politician Lord Taylor of
Warwick (whose parents are Jamaican)*.*

* "Birmingham," Lord Taylor replied.

"
Oh no, I might catch some ghastly disease.
"

Philip, when asked if he wanted to stroke a koala bear during a royal visit to Australia, 1992.

Smashing Fact No.9

Philip calls his wife,
HRH Queen Elizabeth II, a
variation of food-based terms
of endearment, including
"sausage" and "cabbage".

66

Tolerance is the one essential ingredient. You can take it from me that the Queen has the quality of tolerance in abundance.

99

Philip, offering advice for a successful marriage, 1997.

The Gaffer

"

I never see any home cooking –
all I get is fancy stuff.

"

Philip, discussing banquets at Buckingham Palace, 1987.

66

Most stripping is done by hand.

99

Philip, to an 83-year-old Mars bar factory worker, while discussing how she used to strip or cut Mars Bars by hand, 2013.

The Gaffer

" "

Gentlemen, I think it is time we
pulled our fingers out.

" "

*Philip, in a speech to the Industrial Co-partnership
Association on Britain's inefficient industries, 1961.*

"
We did our best.

"

Philip, on parenting, to biographer Gyles Brandreth, 2004.

The Gaffer

"

The impression the public have got is unfair. I've just got to live with it. It happens to a lot of people.

"

Philip, on his public image, to biographer Gyles Brandreth, 2004.

66

I'm not sure how useful it is
to speculate about the future.
Making the most of the present
is quite important.

99

*Philip, discussing the future, to biographer Gyles
Brandreth, 2004.*

The Gaffer

"

I didn't particularly want to go into the Army. I didn't fancy the walking too much.

"

Philip, on joining the Navy, 1942.

" I didn't want a bloody lecture! "

Philip, to the gold-medal-winning garden laid on by Australian celebrity gardener Jamie Durie. The Duke said, "I do like your tree fern." "Actually it's not a tree fern," replied Durie. "It's a member of the cycad family. It's a Macrozamia moorei." The Duke stormed off.

The Gaffer

> **I was most interested to learn that the X-ray goes in one ear and out of the other.**

Philip, after watching a film about ultrasonics at University of London, 1954.

66

Are you Indian or Pakistani?
I can never tell the difference
with you chaps.

99

*Philip, at an embassy reception for Commonwealth
members in Washington, DC, 1990.*

The Gaffer

❝

To work out how to operate
a TV set you practically have
to make love to the thing.
And why can't you have
a handset that people who
are not 10 years old can
actually read.

❞

*Philip, in an interview to mark the 50th anniversary of the
Design Council's Prince Philip Designers Prize, 2009.*

66

You could smuggle a
bottle of gin out of the country
in that artificial foot.

99

*Philip, to comedian Adam Hills, who has
a prosthetic limb, 2009.*

Smashing Fact No.10

Philip was the first member of the Royal Family to be interviewed on television. The date was 29 May 1961, and he discussed Commonwealth Technical Training Week, a scheme for creating more skilled workers in Britain's labour force.

66

It makes you all look like Dracula's daughters!

99

Philip, to pupils dressed in red uniforms at a Reading school, 1998.

The Gaffer

"

In education, if in nothing else,
the Scotsman knows what is
best for him. Indeed, only a
Scotsman can really survive a
Scottish education.

"

*Philip, in a speech to celebrate his appointment as
Chancellor of Edinburgh University, 1953.*

66

If it doesn't fart or eat hay, she isn't interested.

99

Philip, about his horse-loving daughter, Princess Anne, 1970.

The Gaffer

“

I must be the only
person in Britain glad to see
the back of that plane.

”

*Philip, discussing Concorde (he hated the loud noise it made
as it flew daily over Buckingham Palace), 2003.*

66
They're not mating, are they?
99

Philip, while watching two robots colliding at London's
Science Museum, 2000.

The Gaffer

"

The only active sport, which
I follow, is polo – and most of
the work's done by the pony!

"

Philip, discussing his favourite sport, 1965.

66

It looks like the kind of thing
my daughter would bring back
from her school art lessons.

99

*Philip, after having been shown examples of
Ethiopian art, 1965.*

The Gaffer

66

She's got all the right stuff
in all the right places.

99

*Philip, to comedian Russell Brand's plus-one at the Royal
Variety Performance, 2007.*

66

Fuck off – we are talking
about two boys who have
lost their mother.

99

*Philip, incensed, shouting down the phone to Tony Blair's
spin doctors, while discussing Princess Diana's funeral
arrangements, 1997.*

The Gaffer

66
I'm so old I won't be here.
99

*Philip, to Cherie Blair, upon hearing that London had
won the 2012 Olympic bid, 2005.*